THE BUSY BUNK ACTIVITY BOOK

FOR CAMP

BY DANI KATES

All about Me

My name: _____

My age: _____

My height: _____

My Birthday: _____

I'm from: _____

My hair color: _____

My eye color: _____

Camp Name: _____

Camp Location: _____

Favorite Camp Activity: _____

Favorite Camp Food: _____

Favorite Color: _____

Favorite Dessert or Candy: _____

Favorite Song : _____

Favorite Movie: _____

Favorite Game to Play: _____

Message Decoder!

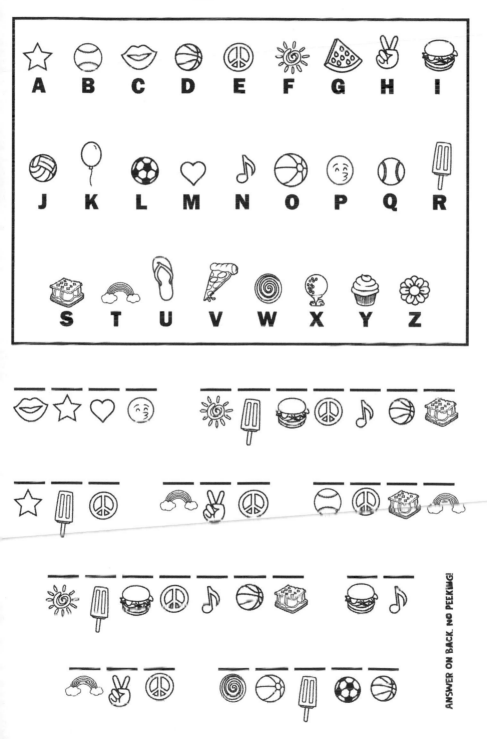

CAMP FRIENDS ARE THE BEST FRIENDS IN THE WORLD

Color these sneakers and find the 8 diferences between the two pictures!

Answers on back of the page, but it's more fun of you don't peek!

1. Different number of stars above the shoes
2. Hearts by the heels are different
3. Ccandy boxes are different, one has more candy circles
4. Emojis are different, one has teeth, one doesn't
5. One of the shoelaces has different dots
6. Ice creams are different, one has less lines
7. only one circle on the bottom shoe
8. Extra star on the toe on the bottom one

Circle the 2 that are the same. Then color of all of them!

Things I've seen at camp that are green...

1. _____
2. _____
3. _____
4. _____
5. _____
6. _____
7. _____
8. _____
9. _____
10. _____
11. _____
12. _____
13. _____
14. _____
15. _____

Decode the words and then unscramble them to reveal the phrase!

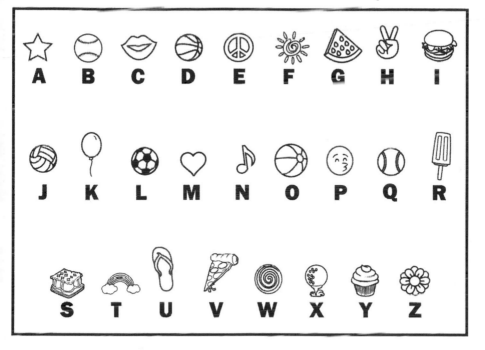

_____ !

LIVE TEN FOR TWO!

COLORING TIC TAC TOE

Player 1 Colors in the X's!
Player 2 Colors in the O's!

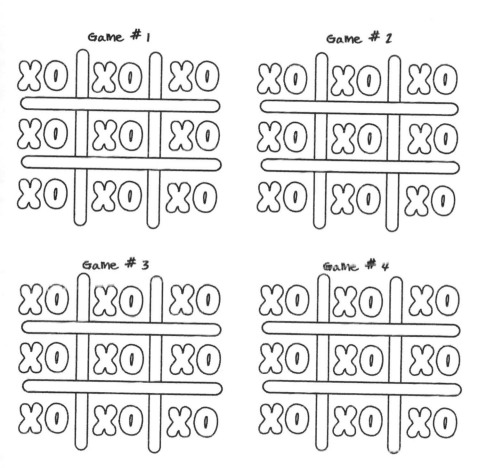

Game #1   Game #2

Game #3   Game #4

And the Winner is...

Game #1   Game #2   Game #3   Game #4

XO   XO   XO   XO

Please bring the boat through the maze to the water!

3D Triple Level Tic Tac Toe

The game is basically the same as regular tic-tac-toe: you try to win by getting three X's or O's in a row.
A diagonal, horizontal, or vertical set of three lets you win.
You can win the regular way-all in one level, or by having 3 x's or O's in the same square on each level,
or by doing 3 in a row, with 1 on each level.

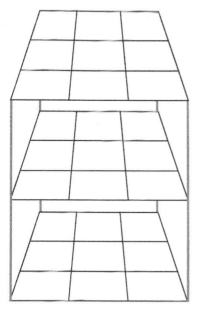
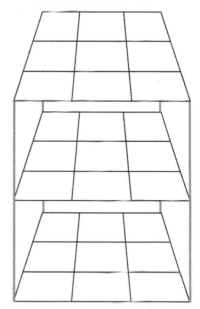
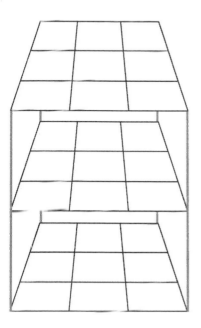
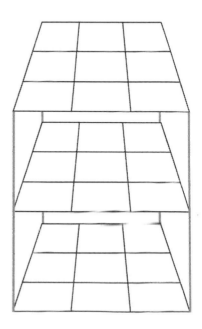

Things I've seen at camp that are Red...

1. _____
2. _____
3. _____
4. _____
5. _____
6. _____
7. _____
8. _____
9. _____
10 _____
11. _____
12. _____
13. _____
14. _____
15. _____

The Dot Game

Players take turns drawing lines that connect 2 dots. When a player draws a line that closes a box, they write their initial inside the box and get to go again. The player with the most closed boxes wins!

Message Decoder!

A	B	C	D	E	F	G	H	I

J	K	L	M	N	O	P	Q	R

S	T	U	V	W	X	Y	Z

YOU ARE GOING TO HAVE THE BEST SUMMER EVER

Draw some Ice Pops and Ice Cream

You dropped your marshmallows!!! You'll need them to make s'mores...
Please use the maze to find them !

COLORING TIC TAC TOE

Player 1 Colors in the X's!
Player 2 Colors in the O's!

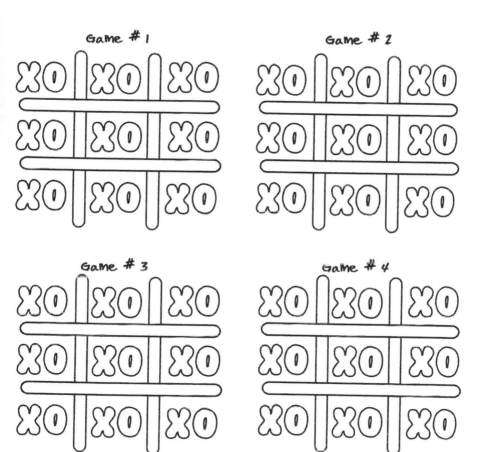

Game #1

Game #2

Game #3

Game #4

And the Winner is...

Game #1   Game #2   Game #3   Game #4

Things I've seen at camp that are Blue...

1. _____
2. _____
3. _____
4. _____
5. _____
6. _____
7. _____
8. _____
9. _____
10. _____
11. _____
12. _____
13. _____
14. _____
15. _____

CONNECT 4 !

Player One draws X's, Player Two draw's O's
Start at the bottom and work your way up.
You may only draw an X or an O in a circle that is above a circle
that already has an X or an O in it.
First player to get 4 in a row (vertical, horizontal, or diagonal) wins!

CAMP ATHLETICS

```
J  I  V  O  L  L  E  Y  B  A  L  L  A  F  E
R  T  E  N  N  I  S  O  F  T  B  A  L  L  S
E  D  A  N  C  E  A  X  X  E  T  D  K  T  S
L  Y  Q  Y  H  A  N  D  B  A  L  L  R  M  O
B  O  B  A  S  E  B  A  L  L  Z  G  E  D  R
A  L  O  K  S  L  L  A  B  T  O  O  F  J  C
S  H  G  N  I  D  A  E  L  R  E  E  H  C  A
K  N  O  T  N  I  M  D  A  B  W  T  R  M  L
E  C  A  P  T  U  R  E  T  H  E  F  L  A  G
T  D  X  C  R  J  K  T  U  G  O  W  A  R  B
B  T  H  G  T  E  U  Q  O  R  C  Q  E  O  S
A  G  Y  L  U  X  N  V  B  B  B  A  K  F  U
L  O  L  O  B  S  W  S  O  C  C  E  R  B  I
L  L  D  S  C  I  B  O  R  E  A  B  M  U  Z
Y  F  I  S  C  I  T  S  A  N  M  Y  G  T  O
```

AEROBICS	CROQUET	SOCCER
BADMINTON	DANCE	SOFTBALL
BASEBALL	FOOTBALL	HANDBALL
BASKETBALL	GOLF	TENNIS
CAPTURETHEFLAG	GYMNASTICS	TUGOWAR
CHEERLEADING	LACROSSE	VOLLEYBALL
		ZUMBA

CONNECT 4 !

Player One draws X's, Player Two draw's O's
Start at the bottom and work your way up.
You may only draw an X or an O in a circle that is above a circle
that already has an X or an O in it
First player to get 4 in a row (vertical, horizontal, or diagonal) wins!

Only two of these hot dogs are the same. Which two?

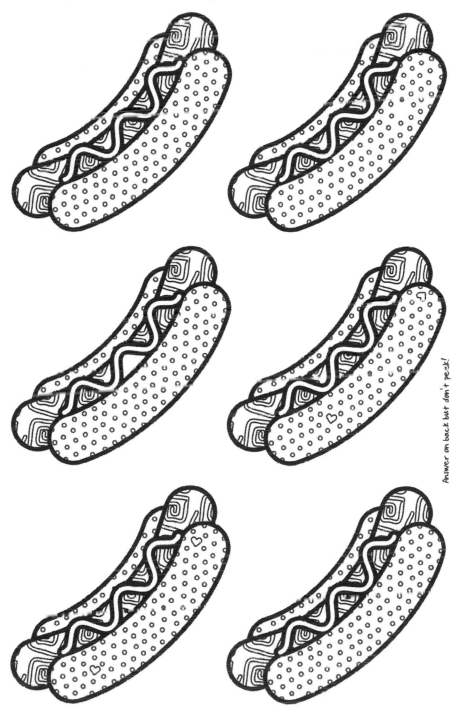

Answer on back but don't peek!

Top left and bottom right are the same.

Oh no! You lost a flip flop!

Help the left one find its way back to
the right one inside the maze!

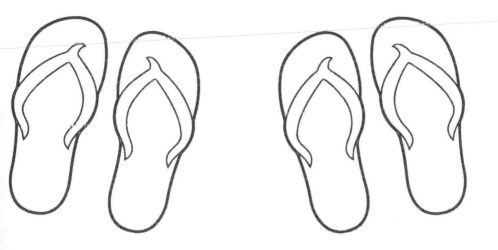

Scavenger Hunt!

Check off each one as you find them! Then write the date and time you found it!

☐ 1. Someone wearing Blue Shorts   Date: _____ Time: _____

☐ 2. Someone wearing a Pink Tank   Date: _____ Time: _____

☐ 3. Someone eating a hot dog   Date: _____ Time: _____

☐ 4. Someone w/ 2 braids in their hair   Date: _____ Time: _____

☐ 5. Someone eating vanilla ice cream   Date: _____ Time: _____

☐ 6. Someone wearing a red swim suit   Date: _____ Time: _____

☐ 7. Someone with a unicorn shirt   Date: _____ Time: _____

☐ 8. A piece of pizza   Date: _____ Time: _____

☐ 9. A popsicle Stick   Date: _____ Time: _____

☐ 10. A rock   Date: _____ Time: _____

☐ 11. A bug   Date: _____ Time: _____

☐ 12. Someone wearing jean shorts   Date: _____ Time: _____

☐ 13. Someone wearing a striped shirt   Date: _____ Time: _____

☐ 14. Someone wearing a pony tail   Date: _____ Time: _____

☐ 16. Someone wearing a white shirt   Date: _____ Time: _____

☐ 17. Someone eating a hamburger   Date: _____ Time: _____

☐ 18. Someone eating cereal   Date: _____ Time: _____

☐ 19. Someone singing a song   Date: _____ Time: _____

☐ 20. Someone making a bracelet   Date: _____ Time: _____

☐ 21. A soccer ball   Date: _____ Time: _____

☐ 22. A basketball   Date: _____ Time: _____

☐ 23. Someone wearing a red hat   Date: _____ Time: _____

☐ 24. A toothbrush   Date: _____ Time: _____

☐ 25. S'mores   Date: _____ Time: _____

☐ 26. A shirt with hearts on it   Date: _____ Time: _____

☐ 27. A chocolate chip cookie   Date: _____ Time: _____

SPOT THE DIFFERENCES. (THERE ARE 10)
(Hint: If you color them in it might be easier to find the differences)

Sports bottle: extra line around the cap
Trunk: Missing heart on the front
Sunglasses: Missing an outline in the heart lens
Shampoo: The emoji has less hair
Ipod: Missing a circle in the button
Ipod: rock and roll is all lowercase
Flip Flops: theres a heart on them
Trunk: Missing tab on the right side
Conditioner: Emoji has eyebrows

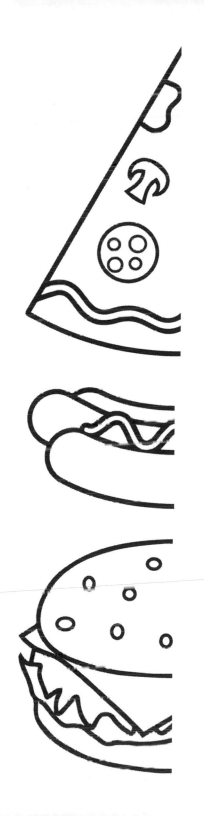

3D Triple Level Tic Tac Toe

The game is basically the same as regular tic-tac-toe: you try to win by getting three X's or O's in a row.
A diagonal, horizontal, or vertical set of three lets you win.
You can win the regular way-all in one level, or by having 3 x's or O's in the same square on each level,
or by doing 3 in a row, with 1 on each level.

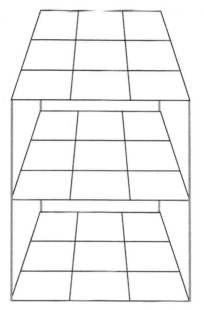

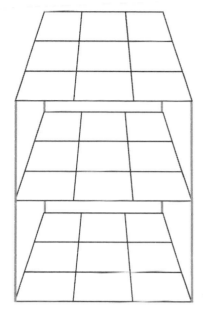

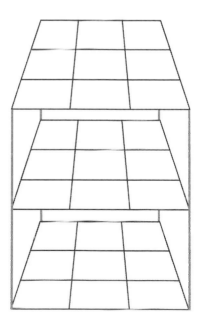

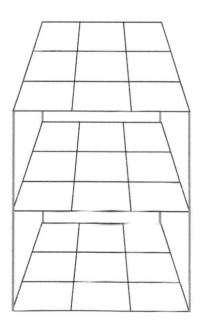

CONNECT 4 !

Player One draws X's, Player Two draw's O's
Start at the bottom and work your way up.
You may only draw an X or an O in a circle that is above a circle
that already has an X or an O in it.
First player to get 4 in a row (vertical, horizontal, or diagonal) wins!

Spot the differences (there are 8) Then color in the pictures!

Answers on back, no peeking!

1. Fire: there is less detail in the top flame
2. Left Ice cream cone: there are sprinkles in the melted part of the top one
3. There is one less marshmallow on a stick in the bottom image
4. Right Ice Cream Cone: top has more spilled ice cream
5. Theres a cupcake on a log in the bottom image
6. One of the marshmallow sticks in the bottom image is shorter in front
7. One of the marshmallow sticks in the top image is shorter in back
8. There's a face in the top flame

The Dot Game

Players take turns drawing lines that connect 2 dots. When a player draws a line that closes a box, they write their initial inside the box and get to go again. The player with the most closed boxes wins!

COLORING TIC TAC TOE

Player 1 Colors in the X's!
Player 2 Colors in the O's!

Game #1   Game #2

Game #3   Game #4

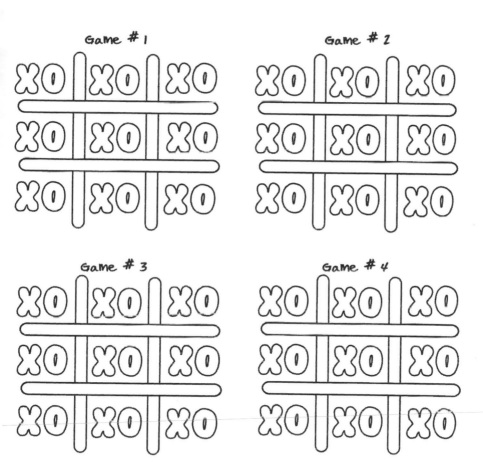

And the Winner Is...

Game #1   Game #2   Game #3   Game #4

Write one word that has to do with camp for each letter!

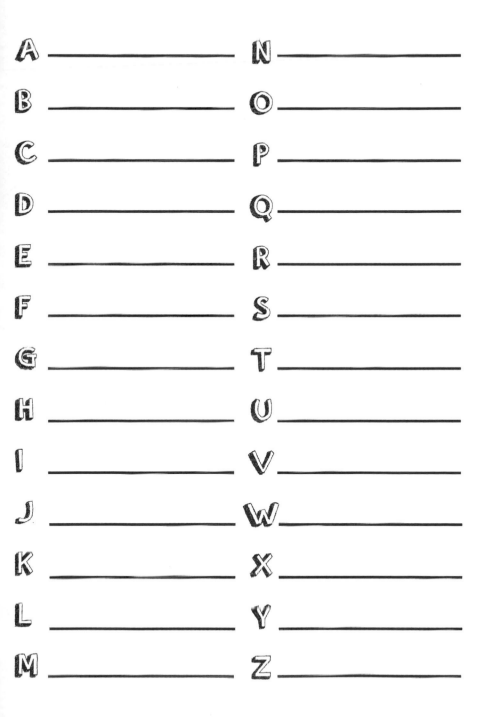

A _____ N _____

B _____ O _____

C _____ P _____

D _____ Q _____

E _____ R _____

F _____ S _____

G _____ T _____

H _____ U _____

I _____ V _____

J _____ W _____

K _____ X _____

L _____ Y _____

M _____ Z _____

STUFF TO PACK FOR CAMP

ACROSS

2. You wear these to sleep
5. You wear these on your feet (for sports)
6. Put this on your bed to keep you warm
9. You wear these in the water
12. Use these to dry yourself
13. Wear these on your feet with sneakers
14. Bring one of these to where when it rains
15. These have two sleeves and you wear them

DOWN

1. Wear these on your feet, without socks
3. These will keep the sun out of your eyes
4. Lay your head on these at night
7. Wear these on your head
8. Use this when it's dark and you need light
10. Bring these to wear when it's cold out
11. Put this on your skin so it doesn't burn
16. Wear these on your bottom half

hangman!

Here is what the HANG-ED MAN should look like!

Cross off incorrect guesses

A E I O U

B C D F G H J
K L M N P Q R
S T V W X Y Z

Make the blanks for your word here

The Dot Game

Players take turns drawing lines that connect 2 dots. When a player draws a line that closes a box, they write their initial inside the box and get to go again. The player with the most closed boxes wins!

3D Triple Level Tic Tac Toe

The game is basically the same as regular tic-tac-toe: you try to win by getting three X's or O's in a row.
A diagonal, horizontal, or vertical set of three lets you win
You can win the regular way-all in one level, or by having 3 x's or O's in the same square on each level,
or by doing 3 in a row, with 1 on each level.

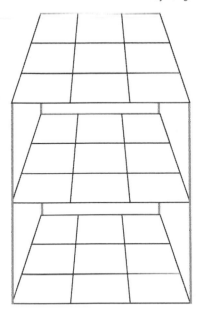
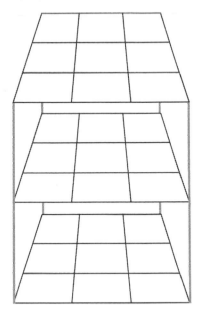
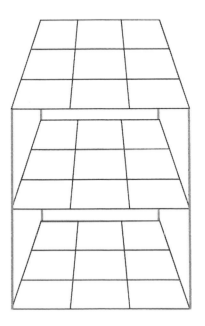
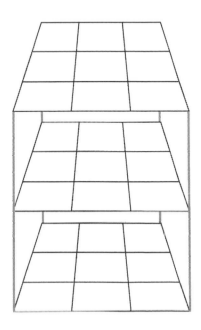

WHAT'S YOUR SUMMER DESSERT NAME?

First Letter of your First name:

A. Silly	J. Sweet	S. Triple
B. Big	K. Sour	T. Salty
C. Crazy	L. Upside-down	U. Giant
D. Amazing	M. Yummy	V. Super
E. Little	N. Cool	W. Awesome
F. Melted	O. Fancy	X. Nice
G. Frozen	P. Fluffy	Y. Half
H. Blue	Q. Tiny	Z. Very
I. Sparkly	R. Double	

First Letter of your Last name:

A. Vanilla	J. Brownie	S. Caramel
B. Chocolate	K. Rainbow	T. Raspberry
C. Almond	L. Sprinkle	U. Kiwi
D. Cherry	M. Peach	V. Sugar
E. Orange	N. Strawberry	W. Mango
F. Pecan	O. Cookie	X. Ginger
G. Cupcake	P. Mint	Y. Banana
H. Marshmallow	Q. Coffee	Z. Berry
I. Fudge	R. Coconut	

Your Birth month:

January: Gelato	May: Popsicle	September: S'mores
February: Ice Cream	June: Sundae	October: Treat
March: Sherbert	July: Cobbler	November: Cone
April: a la Mode	August: Sorbet	December: Icey

DRAW YOUR SUMMER dessert name

(see previous page)

PICTURE SUDOKU!

Solve the Sudoku Puzzles Using Shapes! Color them in when you're done!

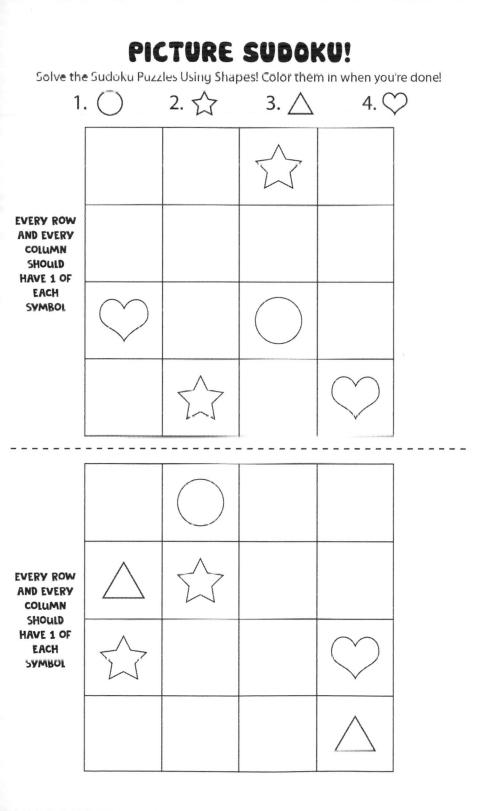

Things I've seen at camp that are gold or yellow...

1. _____
2. _____
3. _____
4. _____
5. _____
6. _____
7. _____
8. _____
9. _____
10 _____
11. _____
12. _____
13. _____
14. _____
15. _____

hangman!

Here is what the
HANG—ED MAN
should look like!

Cross off incorrect guesses

A E I O U

B C D F G H J
K L M N P Q R
S T V W X Y Z

Make the blanks for your word here

CONNECT 4 !

Player One draws X's, Player Two draw's O's
Start at the bottom and work your way up.
You may only draw an X or an O in a circle that is above a circle
that already has an X or an O in it.
First player to get 4 in a row (vertical, horizontal, or diagonal) wins!

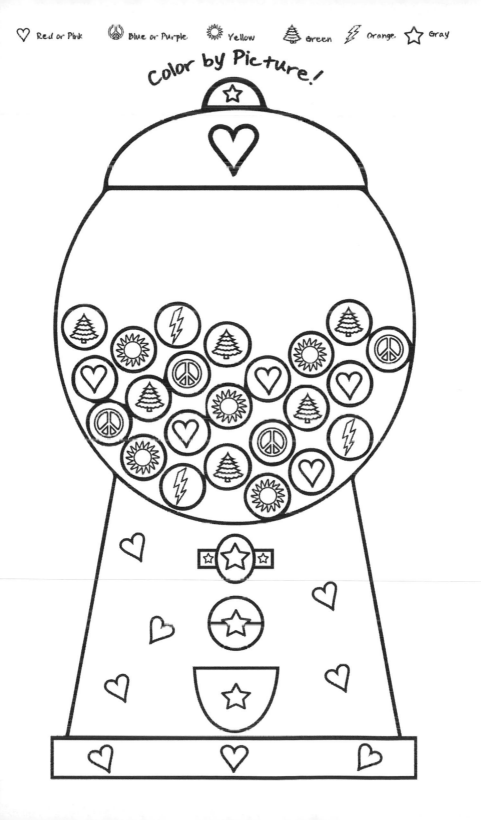

Color by Picture!

Red or Pink   Blue or Purple   Yellow   Green   Orange   Gray

COLORING TIC TAC TOE

Player 1 Colors in the X's !
Player 2 Colors in the O's !

Game # 1

Game # 2

Game # 3

Game # 4

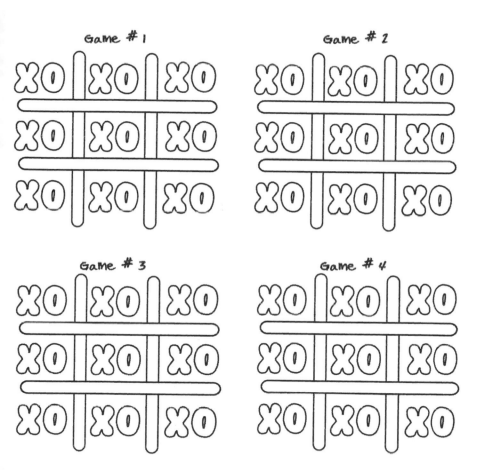

And the Winner is...

Game #1   Game #2   Game #3   Game #4

WORD SCRAMBLE

Unscramble the letters to create camp words! Use the letters
in the shaded boxes to form a new word that answers the riddle!

1. PACM

2. RMUSME

3. KUBN

4. GABRMHREU

5. DSEFINR

6. STPRSO

7. IAICIEVTST

8. LOSROCSENU

9. MEFPCAIR

10. RSMSOE

11. IENNTS

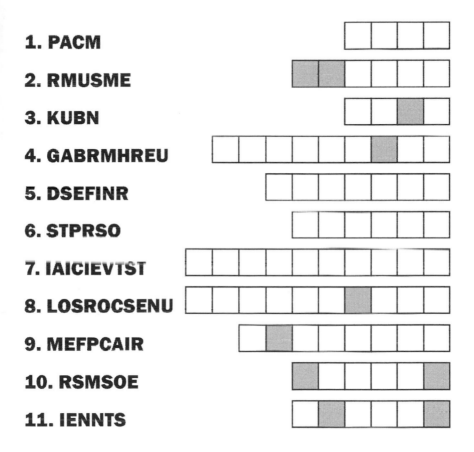

What does the sun drink out of ?

_____

(Answers on back, but don't peek!)

Camp, Summer, Bunk, Hamburger, Friends, Sports,
Activities, Counselers, Campfire, Smores, Tennis

The sun drinks out of SUNGLASSES!

COLORING TIC TAC TOE

Player 1 Colors in the X's!
Player 2 Colors in the O's!

Game #1   Game #2

Game #3   Game #4

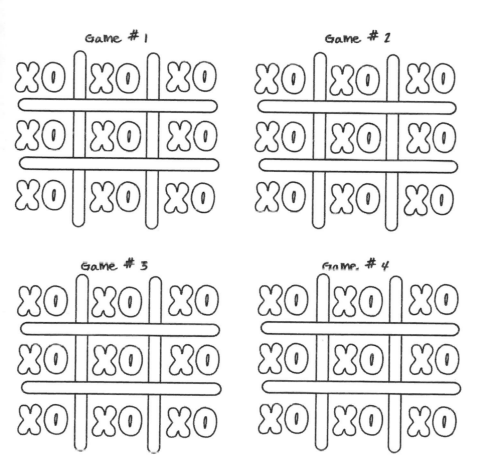

And the Winner is...

Game #1   Game #2   Game #3   Game #4

CAMP COLORING WORD SEARCH
Color in the words as you find them!

```
S P M A C W F P J Z Y L A K E
T I E D Y E G R E E N P F D T
F E S F L L A B Y E L L O V I
A U T S M Y B M C L Y B Y E H
R L U K E U K S E A M B D K W
C B B L N S U A D M O F N I D
D I I K D M S G Y S O F A R L
N E N P M L N A S A I R C R O
A D G E M I O V L I K N I U B
S N R S T U J G R C U I N E R
T S W I M M I N G J N A N E S
R O S D N E I R F H D U S G T
A I Z I D C S O C C E R S U W
V F L I P F L O P S R W H M B
J H F F Z B A W B V T M P A Q
```

CAMP	BFF	WHITE	BLUE
BUNK	LAKE	GOLD	RED
BUS	VISITINGDAY	KAYAKING	GREEN
FRIENDS	FLIPFLOPS	TUBING	MEMORIES
SMORES	TENNIS	TIEDYE	VOLLEYBALL
CANDY	SOCCER	ARTSANDCRAFTS	SUMMER
SUNGLASSES	SWIMMING	COLORWAR	

WORD SCRAMBLE

Unscramble the letters to create camp words! Use the letters
in the shaded boxes to form a new word that answers the riddle!

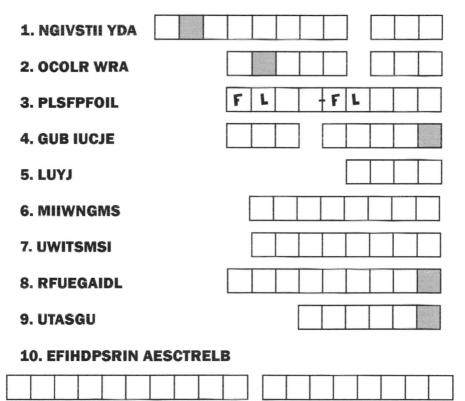

1. NGIVSTII YDA

2. OCOLR WRA

3. PLSFPFOIL F L ☐ ┼ F L ☐ ☐

4. GUB IUCJE

5. LUYJ

6. MIIWNGMS

7. UWITSMSI

8. RFUEGAIDL

9. UTASGU

10. EFIHDPSRIN AESCTRELB

Which letter is the coldest?

___ ___ ___ ___   ___

ANSWERS ON BACK, BUT NO PEEKING!

VISITING DAY, COLOR WAR, FLIPFLOPS, BUG JUICE, JULY, SWIMMING, SWIMSUIT, LIFEGUARD, AUGUST, FRIENDSHIP BRACELETS

THE COLDEST LETTER IS ICED T !

CONNECT 4 !

Player One draws X's, Player Two draw's O's
Start at the bottom and work your way up.
You may only draw an X or an O in a circle that is above a circle
that already has an X or an O in it.
First player to get 4 in a row (vertical, horizontal, or diagonal) wins!

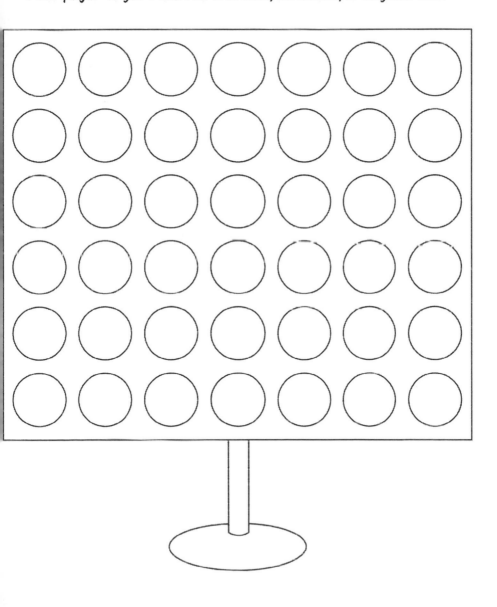

hangman!

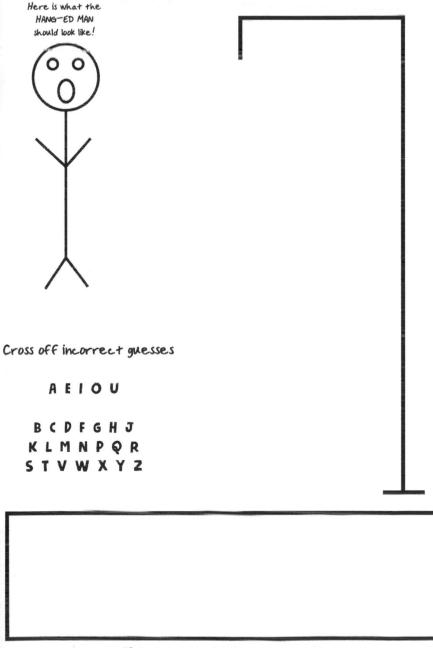

Here is what the
HANG—ED MAN
should look like!

Cross off incorrect guesses

A E I O U

B C D F G H J
K L M N P Q R
S T V W X Y Z

Make the blanks for your word here

Which two S'mores are the same?
Color those 2 the same and the rest differently!

TOP RiGHT AND BOTTOM RiGHT ARE THE SAME!

Only Color the
Foods you Like!

Take a Vote! Ask your friends.
Tally up the points and then write the final # in the boxes

☐ Summer or Winter ☐

☐ Beach or Pool ☐

☐ Lake or Ocean ☐

☐ Ice Cream or Ice Pop ☐

☐ Hamburger or Hot Dog ☐

☐ Pizza or Mac & Cheese ☐

☐ Soccer or Tennis ☐

☐ Tic Tac Toe or Hangman ☐

☐ Dancing or Singing ☐

☐ Smores or Ice Cream Sandwiches ☐

☐ Making Bracelets or Playing Cards ☐

☐ Barefoot or Sandals ☐

☐ Ceramics or Nature ☐

☐ Chocolate or Vanilla ☐

hangman!

Here is what the
HANG—ED MAN
should look like!

Cross off incorrect guesses

A E I O U

B C D F G H J
K L M N P Q R
S T V W X Y Z

Make the blanks for your word here

FUN ACTIVITIES

```
C  V  F  W  T  B  P  F  F  G  Y  T  W  H  B
O  T  P  I  P  D  I  S  C  O  H  P  B  S  S
N  Z  L  G  D  N  U  E  U  G  J  Y  O  C  G
C  O  A  T  R  N  X  H  I  Q  M  V  W  A  J
E  W  Y  M  O  C  A  N  S  Z  Z  Z  L  V  P
R  G  S  M  B  A  O  I  U  F  C  Q  I  E  Y
T  T  Z  F  W  N  J  O  C  S  W  D  N  N  Y
S  C  C  O  I  T  P  G  R  I  B  T  G  G  G
J  M  A  S  Z  E  J  N  I  Y  G  Q  S  E  E
C  P  A  M  L  E  L  I  C  P  K  A  L  R  T
G  C  M  D  P  N  E  B  C  J  Q  B  M  H  C
V  R  K  W  T  F  X  Y  V  Y  T  B  L  U  W
K  F  Y  W  C  O  I  M  Z  Q  S  Q  N  N  E
D  A  M  B  Z  U  J  R  T  C  C  C  Y  T  W
R  P  A  K  T  H  E  M  E  P  A  R  K  S  P
```

PLAYS

CASINO NIGHT

CIRCUS

DISCO

BBQ

MAGICIAN

SCAVENGER HUNT

CAMPFIRE

CANTEEN

CONCERTS

BOWLING

BINGO

THEME PARKS

The Dot Game

Players take turns drawing lines that connect 2 dots. When a player draws a line that closes a box, they write their initial inside the box and get to go again. The player with the most closed boxes wins!

Spot the differences. There are 8.
Then color in the sneakers.

ANSWERS ARE ON THE BACK!

COLORING TIC TAC TOE

Player 1 Colors in the X's !
Player 2 Colors in the O's !

Game # 1

Game # 2

Game # 3

Game # 4

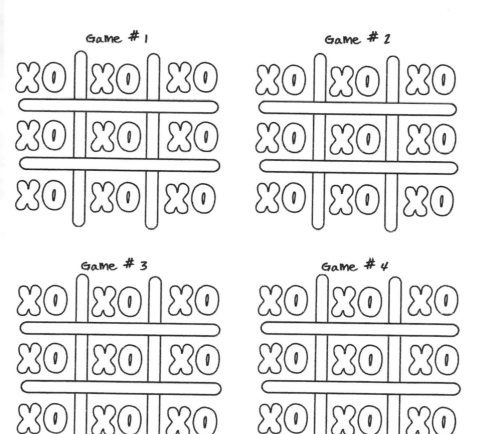

And the Winner is...

Game #1   Game #2   Game #3   Game #4

A REALLY LONG LIST OF ALL EVERYTHING YOU LOVE ABOUT CAMP

You can include friends, counselors, food, activities,
games, memories, songs, and anything else you can think of !

1. _____
2. _____
3. _____
4. _____
5. _____
6. _____
7. _____
8. _____
9. _____
10. _____
11. _____
12. _____
13. _____
14. _____
15. _____
16. _____
17. _____
18. _____
19. _____
20. _____
21. _____
22. _____
23. _____
24. _____
25. _____
26. _____
27. _____
28. _____
29. _____
30. _____

31. _____
32. _____
33. _____
34. _____
35. _____
36. _____
37. _____
38. _____
39. _____
40. _____
41. _____
42. _____
43. _____
44. _____
45. _____
46. _____
47. _____
48. _____
49. _____
50. _____
51. _____
52. _____
53. _____
54. _____
55. _____
56. _____
57. _____
58. _____
59. _____
60. _____